I0469605

5 Laws of Marketing That Every Business Should Live By

www.5lawsofmarketing.com
By Wesley R. Young with Rich Vance

5 Laws of Marketing That Every Business Should Live By

By Wesley R Young
with Rich Vance

www.5lawsofmarketing.com
By Wesley R. Young with Rich Vance

5 Laws Of Marketing That Every Business Should
Live By

Address all inquires to:

Wesley R Young
PO Box 10
Middleport, OH 45760

www.5lawsofmarketing.com
info@5lawsofmarketing.com

This publication is designed to provide accurate
and authoritative information in regard to the
subject matter covered. It is sold with the
understanding that the author is not engaged in
rendering legal, accounting or other professional
services.

ISBN 13: 978-1456558048
ISBN 10: 1456558048

www.5lawsofmarketing.com
By Wesley R. Young with Rich Vance

www.5lawsofmarketing.com
By Wesley R. Young with Rich Vance

That Every Business Should Live By

Acknowledgements

Whenever you complete a work like this there are many people who have contributed to your knowledge over the course of your life. That usually means that you forget to list everyone that you should. Because of this I have only listed a few people below who have had the most recent impact on my work. To everyone else, even if you aren't listed I still appreciate your help along the way.

My family consisting of Jodi, Tori, Madi and mom and dad, my business associate and friend Rich Vance and my friend Randy Ray. My family has always supported my entrepreneurial side and my two friends have always been willing to listen, critique and help me think my way through business challenges. Thank you all from the bottom of my heart.

Why This Book Is So Short

Recently I was having a conversation with a good friend of mine who is a successful businessman. We were talking about a type of how-to book that teaches people how to do a specific thing. There are more ways than one to do this but they all amount to about the same thing. And they all seem to follow the same basic format. Each book tells you what you really need to know in just a few chapters and then has a bunch of other chapters that just make everything more complicated. My question was why every book had to make it so complicated. My friend used an example to illustrate a point. Here is roughly what he said.

It is just like diet books and plans. No matter what diet plan you follow it boils down to burning more calories than you take in. But it is easier to sell a 300-page book than a 3-page book, even if the 3-page book has all of the information you need. So you will find books in just about every non-fiction category that are filled with fluff and extra things that you don't need.

You have realized that this book, the one you are holding in your hands right now, is not very big. The reason for this is because to learn how to instantly start improving your marketing and business doesn't require 300 or more pages of filler. I have left out all of the extra things that you don't need and only included the most important information. This not only makes it quick to read, it also means that you get to spend more time improving your business instead of reading a bunch of boring chapters and that you can get started improving your marketing and making money in just a few hours.

About The Author - (Why you should listen to what I have to say)

The reason I am going to tell you about my past experiences in marketing and business is not to brag, but to show you that I have used in the real world what I am telling you works. I have read too many books that were obviously written by someone who hasn't actually used their own advice in a real business. Of course you don't have to believe that my ideas work, you just need to try them. The only way that you won't profit from the information included in this book is if you don't read it or don't use it after you have read it. These marketing tactics work and you will be able to see it for yourself once you get started. I urge you to put a few of the ideas into action and see the results for yourself before just assuming something won't work. You will be pleasantly surprised, I assure you.

For over 20 years I have been running, buying, selling, creating and consulting with businesses of every shape and size.

www.5lawsofmarketing.com
By Wesley R. Young with Rich Vance

My experience runs from working with businesses doing less than $100,000 in yearly sales to businesses doing over $1 Billion in annual revenues. (Yes, that is Billion with a B). My marketing background includes work with all types of advertising including magazines, newspapers, radio, television and direct mail as well as using social media, e-mail and the Internet. It also includes all of the other things that aren't advertising that are included in marketing. These don't need to be listed here because you are getting ready to learn more about them in this book.

Here is an example of what I have done for businesses that I have been involved with. This is an actual business and the numbers are real, but I am not going to disclose the name of the business to protect them from their competitors. It is a fairly typical retail business. When I started working with them, their yearly sales were just under $1.5 Million with a gross profit of 22%. The big problem was that they were running around 22% of sales as expenses also. If you have been in business long at all you realize that 22% going out and 22% coming in leaves nothing in the profit column. This is also a recipe for disaster because if your cash flow falters you don't have any cushion.

Within two years the business had improved sales to just under $3 Million, improved their gross profit to over 30% and were keeping their expenses at 25% of sales. Not only were we able to double sales, we were also able to create a 5% spread between gross profit and expense percentage. This created a 5% margin in the net profit before taxes column. This is what I do. Create profits that go directly to the bottom line.

Many prospective clients and other people who I talk to that are interested in my services and what I do ask me about my educational background. While I am educated in the business world, holding a Masters degree in Business Administration, I always stress that my real education has come by actually working in a business and learning what works and what doesn't first hand. Most of what I learned in school has not been valuable in the real world. The good thing is I have both areas covered. If a business will only work with an "educated" individual, I fit the bill. On the other hand, if a business is only worried about dealing with a person that has actually made money in the trenches, I fit that bill too. My plan was to cover as many bases as possible. This should be the plan in your business as well.

Other experiences that have helped me prepare to help businesses of all types and size include teaching occasional business courses at the college level, speaking to groups of business people, writing for different business markets and working as a co-host on a business radio show.

You will find many ways to help your business and increase your profits in this book. But if you feel that my services can help you even more, there is information at the back of the book about how to contact me.

My friend, business associate and occasional business partner Rich Vance has also contributed to this book. Here is some additional information about his business experience and background.

He has many years of experience in the business world working with both online and offline marketing. Rich has been heavily involved in the agricultural business for over 20 years, using traditional and non-traditional methods of marketing. He also has experience in the automotive industry with sales and management experience and has worked with retail and commercial accounts with a major retailer.

The past four years he has been working extensively in online marketing and search engine optimization (SEO). Whether working with a start up business or existing business, there are always ways to improve marketing, management or sales practices and his experience allows him to effectively help whichever type of business is in need.

Contact information for Rich Vance can be found at the end of the book.

Law # 1 – Everything Is Marketing

Most business people believe that marketing is advertising. While advertising is a part of marketing, it is only one part. Everything that you do in your business is involved with marketing. From the appearance of your store and employees, to the way you answer the phones to the way your products and services are priced is marketing. Every decision you make and every action completed in your business is either helping your business or hurting it.

Advertising is an important part of your marketing, but even if you have the best advertising in the world but fail in other parts of your business you will still fail. You will just fail faster because your advertising will provide lots of customers to drive away.

Of course most businesses that have survived very long don't get everything wrong. Every business has areas where it can improve, but most businesses do enough right to get by. The best businesses do as many things as they possibly can right because they realize that every customer is an opportunity to build a long-term relationship. Long-term relationships with happy customers lead to increased profit.

The main point of this first section is to help you understand that you need to take a new hard look at every aspect of your business before worrying about your advertising. Make sure you are doing everything you can right so that when your advertising starts sending more prospective customers your way you will be able to make as many of them as possible long term customers.

This book is applicable to just about any type of business I can think of, so there will be things that everyone can use and a few things that you may not be able to use. However, before you say you can't use one of the ideas, make sure that is actually the case. If you are in a service business like carpet cleaning, you may be tempted to ignore any advice directed to the retail industry. You are of course free to pick and choose as you see fit, but if you can figure out a way to make something work in your business, you will just make more money.

For example, the common carpet cleaning business simply runs some advertising in the local newspaper and on the local radio stations, receives calls and schedules appointments, then goes out and cleans the carpets and collects the payment. All of this is well and good, but why not see if there is something else that you can combine with your business to improve your bottom line? You are already in the customer's house, why not offer a service or product line that complements what you do. You are cleaning carpets, so the customer is more than likely interested in a clean house. Could you offer a complete bathroom cleaning and sterilization service? Or can you offer a line of cleaning supplies? What about co-operating with a local contractor who does remodeling, installs windows and builds decks? You can refer customers to each other for a commission.

The point is not just directed at carpet cleaners. Most businesses have hidden opportunities where they can increase their profit. You have to develop the mindset that you will do everything possible to improve your bottom line.

Here is a list of areas to look at in your business. This is not a complete list, just a tool to help you get started. As long as you remember that everything you do and every business decision you make are marketing related, you will quickly start seeing the parts of your business through new eyes.

- The location of your business
- The appearance of your business
- The appearance of your employees
- The way your employees answer the phone

- The way your employees greet customers
- The way your employees handle complaints
- The cleanliness of your business
- Your product mix
- Add on sales opportunities
- Your pricing structure and strategy
- Your customer follow up
- Tracking your customers buying habits
- Building your in house customer list
- The appearance of your web site
- How easy your web site is to use
- All of your advertising including:
- Direct mail
- Online
- Newspaper
- Magazine
- Radio
- Television

To finish up this first law I wanted to cover an area where almost every business can start putting effective marketing into action at very little cost. You need a list of your current and past customers to market to. If you aren't already building your own house list, you must start as soon as possible.

Every business is different, but many already have their customer's information on file. If you don't have a business that already collects this information you may have to offer your customers a small bribe to get their information. This may be as simple as telling them that by joining your list they will receive special offers throughout the year or you can give away a low cost item to everyone who joins.

The power of having your own house list is you can always market to them. If you have a business that has a slow season you can plan ahead and increase your marketing efforts during this time. Once you start seeing how different offers work when going to your house list you can start experimenting with other types of direct mail to an outside list to see if you can make it profitable.

As you gather more information about the customers on your list you can start splitting your list into smaller lists. For example, you can start a second list of customers who spend more money and market to them differently. You can start marketing to customers who shop on a set schedule based on how often they buy. There is a tremendous amount of extra profit that can be taken in almost every business by effectively using a house list.

Once you have built your house list, you should try to stay in contact with your customers at least 12 times a year. 18 to 24 times a year is even better. This keeps you and your business in the front of their mind so the next time they need your products or services they will think of you first.

Law # 2 – Advertising Must Be Trackable, Measurable And Accountable

I almost titled this chapter "Marketing Must Be Trackable, Measurable and Accountable" but after pounding home the idea that marketing is not just advertising in the first chapter I didn't want to make this concept confusing. It can be difficult, if not impossible; to measure the improvement in your business from changing the way your employees answer the phone or some of the other marketing ideas from the first chapter. But where you must track and measure is in your advertising.

Here is a common example of an advertisement that many businesses run and have no idea how effective it is. Open your phone book and take a look at the yellow pages where all of the businesses that have bought advertising have their ads. Find the ads that have a way to track how many customers come through that particular ad. You won't find very many, if you find any at all.

So how does the business owner who placed the ad know if it was a good investment? The answer is that they don't know. If you are going to become a true marketer you have to know. If an ad costs $1,000, it had better at the very least pay for itself or it is a waste of time and money.

Some forms of advertising are easier to track than others, but all types of effective advertising can be tracked. Using the example from above of yellow page ads simply put a coupon that the customer must bring in or offer a discount tied directly to the ad.

This way you can keep track of exactly how many new customers an ad is responsible for and see how much money you actually make because of it. Then when it is time to decide whether to renew an ad or place an ad in a similar type of media you can make an informed decision.

When you don't track the effectiveness of your advertising you are forced to guess at the results. If you want to make as much money as possible, there is no room for guessing. This also lets you test different types of advertising to find the combinations that are most profitable.

How to see if you are really making any money

I really didn't know the best place to put this in the book, but it is so important that I knew it had to be included. It really isn't a marketing thing, but it covers one of the biggest problems I see in businesses I deal with. I ask them if they are making any money and if they can actually give me an answer I ask them how they know. While I don't have anything against accountants, the accounting profession has brought on part of this. When I ask the above questions, I am not asking about the profit statement or balance sheet. What I am asking is more about the health of the business.

Here is a simple way to see if your business is making any money. And this is something that you need to know by the day; week, month and year for as far back as you can track it. If you don't know or aren't tracking it now, you need to start right now. Not tomorrow or next week, but right now.

No matter what type of business you are in, you are selling something. It doesn't matter if it is goods or services. Everything you sell has a cost involved. This is usually called the cost of goods sold, or COGS. For example, if you sell staplers for $10 and you pay $4 for them, your cost of goods sold is $4 per stapler. This leaves a gross profit of $6.

What you need to track is how much gross profit you are generating and compare this number to every dollar that is going out other than COGS. What is left over is your profit before taxes. Now is when you get the accountants involved in order to pay as few taxes as possible on this money.

Some of you may be saying that this is a lot like a cash flow statement. Well, it is much like a cash flow statement, but it also tells me exactly what kind of shape a business is in.

Once you start tracking all of this information, you will realize exactly what can be done to make more money. You either have to increase the money coming in, decrease the money going out or both. The way to increase the money coming in is sell more at the same gross profit percentage, increase the gross profit percentage on the same sales, or increase sales and gross profit percentage at the same time.

Notice that decreasing the money going out does the same thing to the bottom line as increasing the money coming in. Also notice that sales numbers by themselves mean very little. If you are losing a dollar on everything you sell, more sales just means that you are going broke faster.

If you don't take a single thing other than this out of this book, you will be a better business person because of it and you will instantly move to the top few percentage in terms of knowing and understanding your business.

The reason I decided to include this in this chapter is because it deals with tracking. You must track everything if you want to make more money.

The value of a customer

The value of a new customer is not just how much you can make on the first transaction. It includes how much you can make from them over the lifetime of your business relationship with them. If you don't know how much you make on average per customer, you need to find out as fast as you can. Then you need to do everything you can to grow this number just like you are trying to grow your number of new customers.

Many businesses don't look beyond the immediate sale. They have no plan to track the value of a customer just like they don't know how much it costs them to get a new customer. If you follow the advice in this book, you won't be one of these other types of businesses. You will be the type of business that survives and thrives while everyone else struggles and fails.

Ways To Track An Ads Response

Here are some examples of different ways to track advertising. These are not the only ways; so if you come up with something better, by all means use it. And feel free to send me examples of ways that you develop to track your marketing. I always appreciate receiving new effective methods.

Coupons that must be presented at the time of purchase are great because not only can you keep them for your tracking you also are getting the customer more involved. They have to either cut the coupon out or take the whole marketing piece with them. They will carry it around until stopping in your store.

Tracking or control numbers on ads or direct mail pieces. These work well if you receive orders by phone. You simply ask the customer for the number listed in the ad. It is always best to tie them to an offer, call to action or discount. Then you can tell the customer when you ask for the number that you are making sure they receive the proper discount, offer or whatever.

You can also say in your advertisement that they must mention the ad to receive the discount or special offer. The biggest problem with this will be getting your employees to correctly track response.

If you are using direct mail and are receiving orders by mail, you can add a suite number to your address or use different names for your reply address.

Many businesses think they can track their marketing by simply asking customers where they heard about the business or something like that. The problem with this is once again your employees will not track this correctly and many customers won't tell you or won't remember. It is not accurate enough for your purposes.

When you are doing radio advertising you almost are forced to tie a specific discount that they have to mention to receive or a specific response code they have to use. Television works much the same way. If you are receiving all of your response by phone you can set up and use different phone numbers for different ads. This can be expensive so this is only a consideration if you are doing a large volume of profitable business from your ads.

If you are using Internet based advertising there are tracking software programs that can be used to see where the traffic comes from and you can also assign different tracking numbers to different types of ads placed online.

Law # 3 – Long Term Marketing Must Be At A Positive Cost

This may seem like a common sense statement, but many businesses are shooting in the dark. Of course this ties in with the previous chapter, but one of your goals should be finding advertising opportunities that consistently bring in more money than they cost. Then you want to use these opportunities for as long as they remain profitable.

One of the easiest examples to understand is direct mail, but the same concepts work with any type of advertising.

In direct mail you have a set cost. Your cost includes the cost of the list you are using, postage, envelopes, labor and whatever materials you are sending the potential customer. If you are sending out 1,000 pieces of mail and your total cost is $1,000, then you know that each piece costs $1 and you must make at least $1,000 in profit from the mailing to break even.

If you are offering a product or service that has a profit of $100, you need to sell at least 10 to break even. The math is pretty simple, but it is also powerful.

When you mail 1,000 pieces and are able to break even, you can then work on different parts of the mailing to increase your response. Continuing with the example above, if you can just improve your sales by one, from 10 to 11, you have made the campaign profitable.

You also need to track and consider the lifetime value of a new customer. Depending on your product or service, how much more can you sell a new customer over the next year and the lifetime of the relationship? You don't have to increase your response (though you will always be trying to increase your response) in the above example if you know that within the next year you can make an average of an additional $50 per new customer. Your break-even point of 10 sales has really been a profit because 10 times $150 is $1500. This would be a very successful mailing campaign. You would want to mail the rest of the available list as quickly as possible with these types of results.

This book is not about direct mail so I won't be covering it in much depth, but in my experience most businesses can profit from using it. Some of the things you must consider are where you will be getting a list to mail to and the size of the available list. You can start with your in house list, which is a list of your current customers, but there are other lists available. There are people who sell lists called list brokers that cover just about any interests and locations you can think of.

The important thing to take from the discussion so far in this chapter is how you can use the direct mail example to apply to all of your advertising. No matter what media you are using, learn if it is working at a profit, figure out how to make it more profitable and find other areas where you can advertise at a profit. The same concepts work with newspaper advertising, radio and television advertising and online advertising.

Here are some common things you can change in your advertisements to try to improve response along with some general rules for your ads. It isn't a complete list. If you are interested in more advanced ad improvement options, research copywriting information from someone who does a lot of direct marketing.

Testing is tracking two different ads that are the same except for one thing. For example two ads that are identical except for the headline. You should test ads as much as you can to find the ones that have the best return.

- Always have a call to action. Tell the customer exactly what you want them to do.
- Try to build a sense of urgency into your ads. Make the customer want to

do it right now. The longer they wait before taking action the less likely you are to get their business.

- Headlines are important and are usually worth testing. The first thing to change is your headline if you are trying to boost response.

- Using pictures in an ad can also boost response if you have room. This is another thing to test. Try an ad with a picture and without. You can also test different pictures.

- If you are using a sales letter format, it is important to keep your sentences and paragraphs short. It is easier for the potential customer to read and they are more likely to finish it.

- Though you have to be careful with this and it only works in certain sales environments, you can test different price points. This works well with direct mail. What you want to avoid is people finding out that you are selling the same thing at two different prices. You can test this at different times or in different locations.

Law # 4 – Use Technology In Your Marketing – But Use It Wisely

With each passing year there seems to be more and more technology in the world. And things seem to be moving faster than ever before. This is a trend that will probably continue as long as the world stays in the same general shape as it is currently in.

This means there is always some new, better, flashier, shinier thing that you can use to help your business. These are not always bad things, but they are not always good things either.

Developments over the past 10 or so years include the Internet, web sites, e-mail, social media like Facebook and Twitter, smaller and smaller cell phones, computers and handheld devices that do more than ever before and a whole list of other things.

There are very few of these things that every business can and / or should use, but you need to consider which ones can help you. You need to look at them with the same eye that you look at any form of marketing and advertising. In other words, is this something that is going to make me money or cost me money?

The one thing on the list above that has reached the point where I feel every business needs one is a web site. It doesn't have to be big or fancy, but if your business doesn't have a web site you are losing potential customers. Here is what you should have at the very minimum.

Your web site should include information about your business including how to contact you, where you are located, what you do and what products and / or services you offer, your hours of operation and anything else that you feel including would help your business gain new customers. Just like any other form of advertising, you need something on your web site that customers can mention, print off and bring in or sign up for. Your web site has to be trackable just like any other form of advertisement.

Many people learn how to build their own web sites, buy their own domain name and set up their own hosting. There is a learning curve involved with this, and if you don't feel comfortable with the entire process, you can hire someone to do it all for you. Just make sure you know exactly what you are getting before hiring anyone to build your web site. My company does offer this service; so see the final chapter about how to contact me if you are interested.

Of course there are plenty of web sites where you can buy just about anything you can think of. Is your business one that could profit from selling things online? These types of web sites are more challenging to set up and get to work right, but the upside is that you can transform a local business into a global business in a very short period of time. Unless you have quite a bit of experience with web design and search engine optimization (SEO), which is the process of getting your pages to rank high in the search engines like Google and Yahoo, you probably need professional help to start selling online. Once again, you need to closely investigate the cost and profit potential before investing in an online transformation for your business. But it can be profitable for the right types of businesses and worth considering.

E-mail is another area of fairly new technology that you should consider using. On the plus side, it is an inexpensive way to communicate with your customers, but on the negative side, most people receive too much e-mail now and tend to not open all of it. I do use e-mail in some of my businesses, but not as the only way to communicate with my customers. Just like social media like Twitter, it does have its place but if it is the only thing you use you are at the mercy of something you can't control.

For example, many businesses used to use fax machines in their marketing. Then there were laws passed greatly restricting the use of faxes so overnight a large marketing avenue was gone. Don't ever let your marketing fall into this type of trap. No matter which type of advertising or marketing is the most profitable, use any and all avenues that are profitable in order to protect yourself and your business.

Law # 5 – Branding Is Always A By-Product Of Marketing, Never The Purpose

This is the shortest chapter in the book, but it can save you more money than any of the others. Branding is a popular word thrown around in many books about business and in many college business courses. It is the process of creating a brand like Pepsi or Nike or Amazon. While there is nothing wrong with building your brand, you must never build your brand without tying it directly to a profit producing action.

Many of the big advertising agencies who charge thousands of dollars and more stress the importance of branding because they know that in a normal branding campaign you have no way of knowing if their services are worth what you are paying. You can't track branding.

Now don't get me wrong, having a strong brand is valuable. But building a strong brand needs to always be tied to cost effective advertising and actions. Feel free to build brand in all of your ads, but make sure you do it while running the types of ads you have learned about here. If the ad isn't trackable you are fighting a losing battle.

And no matter what you do, don't ever use a big advertising agency without talking to me, or someone who knows the type of marketing I have talked about in this book, beforehand. You will more often than not just be throwing money away.

The example I always use of stupid branding is many of the commercials you see on television, especially during big events like the Super Bowl. Whenever you see a commercial, as soon as it is over ask yourself if you know what they sell. Of course many commercials do tell you what they sell, but I can't count how many times I have seen commercials and don't even know what they do afterward.

Then start seeing if there is any way the advertisers can track the effectiveness of their commercials. 99% of the commercials on television have no way to track response. How in the world do they know if the millions of dollars they are sinking into television is worth it?

Of course now I don't have to worry about any of you falling into this trap, because after reading this book you know better. But you are in the minority and will remain there. Which is a good thing. It just means that you will be one of the few with the knowledge and ability to continue to profit.

Building a brand name is a long and often very expensive undertaking. That is why it is so important to always combine your brand building with effective advertising and marketing.

When Amazon.com was launched they had to spend millions of dollars on branding because no one was searching for the word "Amazon" when they were looking for books online. Of course now it is almost a household name, but it was a real struggle at the beginning to earn the brand recognition.

The bottom line is that the majority of us don't have the time or money required to build the type of brand that Amazon has built. But we do have the ability to build our brand while being profitable, and that is the smarter route to take.

No Strings Attached Free Chapter Offer

Every reader of this book will receive a free bonus chapter titled "The Top 10 Free And Low Cost Marketing Strategies" by simply requesting it. You don't have to send any money or sign up for a free trial of anything. Simply mail your request including your name and address to the address below and I will send you the free chapter by first class mail, no strings attached.

Wesley R. Young
PO Box 10
Middleport, OH 45760

The free chapter will also include examples of marketing plans that can be formatted to use in a wide range of businesses as an added bonus.

Unadvertised Second Bonus Offer

To receive a second free unadvertised bonus, go to the web site tied to this book at **www.5lawsofmarketing.com** and click on the link on the side of the page that says "Unadvertised Bonus". You will receive a second free chapter titled "7 Deadly Retail Sins – and what you can do to fix them now!"

Even if you don't have a retail business, this chapter contains some excellent advice for any type of business. And it is free, so why not take advantage right now?

Consulting, Speaking, Services and Training Opportunities

Consulting, speaking, training and services are available for a wide range of businesses. Here is just a small sampling of things that I do. If you think I may be able to help you make more money, please see the next chapter to learn how to contact me.

Consulting:

        Marketing
        Profitability
        Internet sales and transition
        Inventory management
        Pricing strategies
        Customer service
        Direct mail
        Advertising
        Copywriting

Speaking:

> Short, medium and long programs
> from sales meetings and dinner
> engagements to multi-day
> conferences.

Services:

> Marketing plan creation
> Web site design
> Search engine optimization (SEO)
> Complete marketing solutions
> Web site management
> Newsletter creation
> Content generation

Training:

> Marketing
> Sales
> Retail
> Service
> SEO
> Web site

www.5lawsofmarketing.com
By Wesley R. Young with Rich Vance

How To Contact The Author

If you have comments about the book, are looking for a speaker for your next business event or are interested in any of the services offered by the author, you can contact me by mail at the following address or by email. Correspondence for Rich Vance can also be sent to the same address.

Wesley R. Young
PO Box 10
Middleport, OH 45760

info@5lawsofmarketing.com

If you wish to speak about working with me by phone, include detailed information about your business, what you are interested in, your phone number and the best times to reach you.

Introducing the Marketing and Profitability newsletter brought to you by the authors of this book. You now have the opportunity to subscribe to receive a newsletter by mail every month packed full of marketing, profitability and money making tips, tricks and strategies.

Plus every month you also receive a CD with additional content that you can listen to at home or in your car, or copy it over to your I-pod or mp3 player for listening anywhere.

This newsletter includes tactics for every type of entrepreneur and business. And the best part is that it costs less than a cup of coffee a day. If you get just a single thing to help improve your business in an entire year it will easily pay for itself. For complete details see the web site at:

www.marketingandprofitability.com

Notes

Notes

Notes

Notes

Notes